My First Encyclopedia

Editorial

Pat Hegarty • Helen Keith • Amanda Askew

Moira Butterfield • Tony Potter

Illustrated by Jonathan Higham • Jo Moore

Designed by Alyssa Peacock

Visit our website at:
www.autumnchildrensbooks.co.uk

All about the United Kingdom

The United Kingdom, or UK for short, is an island country off the northwest coast of mainland Europe. The UK is made up of Great Britain – comprising England, Scotland and Wales – and Northern Ireland.

Where in the world are we?

WALES

Wales is in the west of mainland Britain. The mountains of Snowdonia are in North Wales and in the south there are hills, valleys and plains. About a fifth of Wales is National Park – beautiful countryside that anyone can visit. Cardiff is its capital city.

People live on some of the islands off the coast of Scotland.

SCOTLAND

Scotland is in the north of Britain. There are mountains, beautiful moorlands, lakes, or 'lochs', and islands such as the Shetlands and the Orkneys. Edinburgh is its capital city.

NORTHERN IRELAND

Northern Ireland is in the northeast of mainland Ireland. Belfast is its capital. It includes the Mourne Mountains, deep river valleys called the Glens of Antrim and Britain's largest lake, Lough Neagh.

ENGLAND

England is in south and central mainland Britain. Its highest hills are the Pennines in the north. The south is low-lying. In the southwest there is a long peninsula – land jutting out into the sea. England's capital is London, which is also the capital of the United Kingdom.

SEA NATION

The United Kingdom has 17,820 km (11,073 miles) of shoreline, and around its coast there are over 1,000 islands. No spot in the country is further than 113 km (70 miles) from the sea.

The English Channel separates England from France by just 32 km (20 miles) at its narrowest point.

ANIMALS OF BRITAIN

Britain is home to lots of land animals, sea creatures and birds. Here are a few of them.

Red deer

The red deer is Britain's biggest mammal. It lives in woodland and on moors. The male red deer, called a stag, grows large antlers.

Field vole

Britain's commonest mammal is the tiny field vole. There are thought to be about 75 million in the country! Voles live in fields and hedgerows, nibbling on grass.

Wren

Britain's commonest bird is the little wren. It has brown feathers and a short stubby tail. Although it is small, it can sing loudly.

Grey seal

Grey seals live around Britain's coast. The best time to see them is in the autumn, when they have baby seal pups.

River fish

Salmon, roach and dace are among the many types of fish found in Britain's rivers.

A brief history

750 BC–43 AD

The Iron Age, when Celtic tribes lived across Britain in thatched huts grouped into villages.

410

Roman forces left Britain, and tribes from the areas now called Germany, Denmark and Holland began settling in England. They are known as the Anglo-Saxons.

878

Alfred, the Anglo-Saxon King of Wessex, defeated the Vikings at the Battle of Edington, and then began to push them back from southern England.

Around 3100 BC

Stonehenge was built, though humans had been living in the British region for much longer – probably about 700,000 years.

43–410 AD

The Romans invaded England and Wales. They ruled this area until the fall of the Roman Empire, but never conquered Scotland.

793

Vikings from Scandinavia began to attack the coast, stealing goods and enslaving people. They eventually invaded parts of Britain.

1066

French Normans invaded, defeating King Harold at the Battle of Hastings. William, Duke of Normandy became King of England.

1455–1485

The Wars of the Roses; civil wars to claim the English throne, between followers of two noble families, the Lancastrians and the Yorkists.

1534

Henry VIII declared himself head of the Church of England, beginning a split with the Roman Catholic Church. It led to centuries of religious conflict.

925

King Alfred's grandson, Athelstan, became the first king of all England.

1215

English King John was forced to sign the Magna Carta, a set of laws that took away some of the monarch's powers.

1485

Lancastrian Henry Tudor defeated Yorkist King Richard III at the Battle of Bosworth and was crowned King Henry VII.

1558–1603

Elizabeth I reigned as English monarch. In 1588 the Armada, a fleet of Spanish ships, tried to invade but were defeated.

1603

Queen Elizabeth's successor, King James I, was the first king to rule over England and Scotland.

1642-51

The English Civil War; when Parliamentarians under Oliver Cromwell beat the Royalist forces of Charles I, who was beheaded in 1649.

1825

The Stockton and Darlington Railway opened – the first steam-powered public railway in the world. Railways then spread across the country.

1837-1901

Queen Victoria ruled over Britain and the British Empire, which included countries such as India, Australia and Canada.

1660-1700s

Charles II returned to rule the country. The years that followed were a time of scientific discovery and new building, now called the Age of Reason.

1666

Parts of London were burned down in the Great Fire. Sir Christopher Wren designed many of the new buildings, including St Paul's Cathedral.

1914-1918

World War I. British forces joined with others to fight Germany and its allies in parts of Europe, the Middle East and Africa.

1939-45

World War II. Britain joined forces with other Allies to defeat Germany, Japan and Italy.

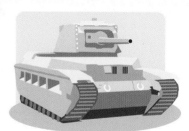

1700s

The Industrial Revolution began – an era when many new factories and industries developed.

1799-1815

British forces fought Napoleon's French armies in Europe, during the Napoleonic Wars. Napoleon was finally defeated at the Battle of Waterloo in 1815.

1953

Elizabeth II was crowned Queen.

2012

The Summer Olympics take place in London and other cities in the UK.

1973

The United Kingdom joined the European Union (EU). Its members work together to make it easier for countries to trade and for people to move around freely.

Famous people from the United Kingdom

Britain has produced lots of important historical figures. Here are just a few who are known all over the world.

SCIENTISTS AND INVENTORS

Sir Isaac Newton

Scientist and maths genius of the late 1600s, who first explained how gravity worked.

Charles Darwin

Naturalist who published his theory of evolution in 1859, explaining how life developed on Earth.

Isambard Kingdom Brunel

Brilliant Victorian engineer who designed and built bridges, railways and ships.

HEROES AND HEROINES

Horatio Nelson

Naval hero whose ships defeated Napoleon's fleet at the Battle of Trafalgar in 1805.

Florence Nightingale

Nurse who organised care for soldiers during the Crimean War in the 1850s and helped found modern nursing.

Sir Winston Churchill

British Prime Minister during World War II.

ENTERTAINERS

Charlie Chaplin

Early 20th century star of silent movies, famous for his shabby suit, bowler hat and cane.

The Beatles

1960s pop group formed by John Lennon, Paul McCartney, Ringo Starr and George Harrison.

WRITERS AND ARTISTS

William Shakespeare

Elizabethan playwright and poet whose work is world famous.

J. M. W. Turner

English 19th-century artist famous for his vivid landscapes and sea views.

J. R. R. Tolkien

Author of the Lord of the Rings trilogy, written in the early 1900s.

SPORTSPEOPLE

Sir Bobby Charlton

English footballer who played for Manchester United. A member of England's winning World Cup team in 1966.

Dame Ellen MacArthur

British yachtswoman who broke the world record for the fastest solo circumnavigation of the globe, in 2005.

UK rock bands have fans in many countries.

English Premier League football is shown on TV all over the world.

Did you know?

Here are some interesting facts about the United Kingdom and the people who live there.

LAND FACTS

✦ The UK covers 241,590 sq km (93,278 sq miles).

✦ The highest mountain in the UK is Ben Nevis in Scotland. It is 1,344 metres (4,408 feet) high.

✦ The longest river in the UK is the Severn, flowing for 354 km (220 miles) through Wales and the west of England.

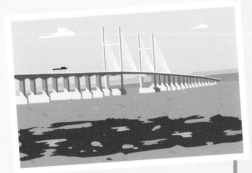

FOOD FACTS

Here are just a few of the many traditional foods found around the UK.

✦ **Haggis** – Scottish dish made from offal.

✦ **Lavabread** – Welsh seaweed fried with oatmeal.

✦ **Lancashire hotpot** – lamb stew.

✦ **Soda bread farl** – a soft, fluffy Irish bread made with baking soda.

PEOPLE FACTS

✦ 61.8 million people live in the UK.

✦ London is the capital city. It is home to 8 million people.

✦ The British Government is based in the Houses of Parliament in London. There are regional government assemblies in Wales and Scotland.

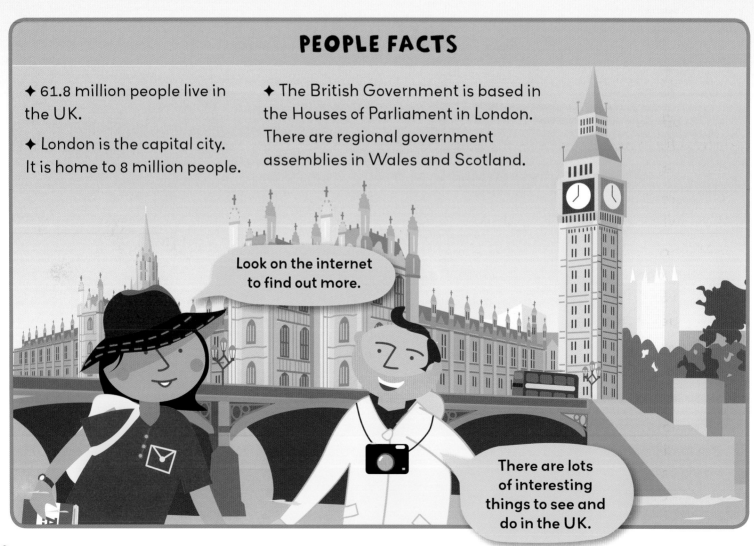

Look on the internet to find out more.

There are lots of interesting things to see and do in the UK.

FESTIVALS

Here are a few of the many yearly events and national holidays that take place in the UK.

✦ **March/April:** Easter, a holiday to commemorate the death and rebirth of Jesus, in the Christian faith. Traditional Easter foods include chocolate eggs and hot cross buns.

✦ **May 1st:** May Day, to celebrate the start of spring. Celebrations include dancing around a maypole and crowning a May Queen.

✦ **September:** Harvest festival, a celebration to give thanks for a successful harvest. Food parcels are given to the elderly and those in need.

✦ **November 5th:** Bonfire Night. Bonfires and firework displays to commemorate the foiling of a plot, led by Guy Fawkes, to blow up the Houses of Parliament in 1605.

✦ **December 25th:** Christmas Day, to celebrate the birth of Jesus, in the Christian faith. Traditional Christmas Day foods include turkey and Christmas pudding.

FLAGS OF THE UK

✦ The official flag of Great Britain is the Union Jack, which is red, white and blue.

✦ Different nations of the UK have their own flags.

✦ The Scottish flag has the x-shaped cross of Saint Andrew on a blue background.

✦ The Welsh flag has a red dragon on white and green.

✦ The flag of England has the red cross of Saint George on white.

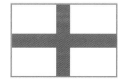

THINGS MADE IN THE UK

Here are a few of the many things produced in the UK.

✦ Food produced by farmers and processed in food factories.

✦ Natural gas and oil from beneath the sea around Britain.

✦ Machinery used on aeroplanes, ships and vehicles.

✦ Medicines and medical equipment.

✦ Creative products such as movies, TV shows, books and music.

✦ Traditional crafts such as weaving and pottery.

Planet Earth

Earth is made up of four layers: the crust, mantle, outer core and inner core. The deeper you go, the hotter it gets – at the centre of the Earth, temperatures are a scorching 7,200 °C!

EARTH'S STRUCTURE

The Earth's crust, which carries all the rocks and minerals, soil and water, is about 40 km (25 miles) thick. You would have to travel another 6,400 km (4,000 miles) to get to the centre of the Earth!

In the mantle, temperatures are high enough to melt rock, forming magma. The Earth's crust floats on the magma as huge slabs, known as 'tectonic plates'. These move 2–5 centimetres a year.

Volcanoes – where magma forces its way through the Earth's crust as a 'volcanic eruption'. Sometimes, clouds of ash and gases are released, too.

Earthquakes – when the edges of two tectonic plates get stuck, then slip with a sudden 'jerking' movement.

Tsunamis – when earthquakes occur under the sea and cause waves, which spread across the oceans. When they reach land, they rush in as a huge, destructive wall of water.

The tallest mountain in the world, Everest, stands at 8,848 metres (29, 029 feet). It is part of the Himalayan mountain range, which formed when tectonic plates collided, forcing the land upwards.

Millions of years ago, slow-moving glaciers carved steep peaks, valleys and lakes.

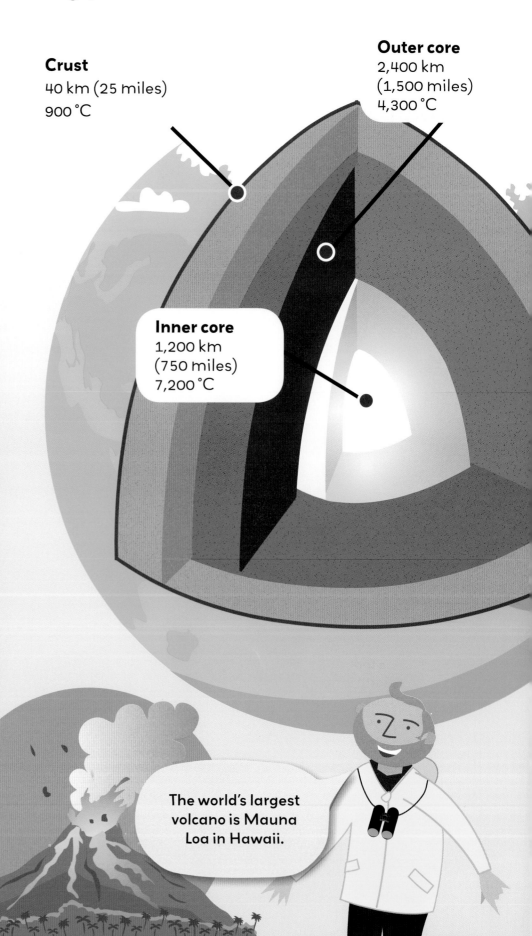

Crust
40 km (25 miles)
900 °C

Outer core
2,400 km
(1,500 miles)
4,300 °C

Inner core
1,200 km
(750 miles)
7,200 °C

The world's largest volcano is Mauna Loa in Hawaii.

CONTINENTS

 The seven continents: Asia, Africa, North America, South America, Antarctica, Europe and Oceania.

Antarctica is classed as a desert, because very little rain or snow falls there. In fact, it is the largest desert in the world.

Mantle
2,800 km
(1,750 miles)
3,700 °C

OCEANS

More than 70% of the Earth is covered by ocean. It is sub-divided into five oceans: the Atlantic, Pacific, Indian, Southern and Arctic and many smaller seas.

The deepest point is the Marianas Trench in the Pacific Ocean. The bottom is 10,923 metres (35,838 feet) below the waves.

BIOMES

 Different types of habitat are called biomes.

Tundra – the coldest biome, with only a few plants and animals able to survive the icy conditions and long, dark winters.

Coniferous forest – covers the largest land area. It is cool with mainly evergreen trees. It stretches across much of Russia, Canada and Scandinavia.

Temperate forest and grassland – covers most of Europe, America and East Asia where winters are mild. Much of the forest has been cleared for farming, roads and houses.

Mediterranean scrub – gets so hot and dry that there are often fires.

Desert – the driest, hottest biome. The few plants and animals living there survive with very little water.

Desert

Savannah – hot and dry, with long grasses and few trees. Found in Africa, Central America and northern Australia.

Tropical forest – hot, dense forests with lots of rain. Found near to the equator.

Ocean – the world's largest biome, teeming with life.

Lakes and rivers – home to many plants and animals.

Tropical rainforests are home to over half the world's plant and animal species.

Dinosaurs and prehistory

Scientists believe that the world is around 4.6 billion years old. Earth has changed a lot, and has been through many stages. Imagine all the things that have happened on Earth over time!

PANGAEA

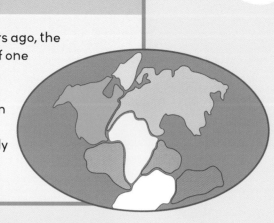

Until 250 million years ago, the world was made up of one land mass, Pangaea, surrounded by a huge ocean, Panthalassa. 200 million years ago, Pangaea split into two continents, before gradually dividing into the continents we know today.

APES AND HUMANS

Human ancestors started life as apes, about 10 million years ago. Over millions of years, the apes became more upright and intelligent, with bigger brains. Eventually they evolved into humans.

As apes evolved into humans, they became better at communicating.

DINOSAURS

Dinosaurs lived hundreds of millions of years ago, in a time called the Mesozoic era. Palaeontologists – scientists who study prehistory – divide the Mesozoic era into three periods: Triassic, Jurassic and Cretaceous.

Types of dinosaur

There were many types of dinosaur, and not all of them lived at the same time. The famous T. rex was from the Cretaceous period. It was a carnivore, or meat-eater, that stood upright on two powerful legs and had lots of very sharp teeth.

Dinosaurs were not the only animals to live before or during the Mesozoic era. There were also:

✦ Pterosaurs – flying reptiles

✦ Primitive crocodiles – whose descendents are still alive today

✦ Plesiosaurs – sea reptiles

✦ Ichthyosaurs – sea reptiles

✦ Mosasaurs – sea-living lizards

✦ Synapsids – reptiles that were similar to modern-day mammals

Most of the dinosaurs died out around 65 million years ago. Scientists think that an asteroid hit Earth and caused changes to the environment that killed dinosaurs and other prehistoric animals.

Some scientists think that a few theropods survived and evolved into modern-day birds.

Clues to the past

Archaeologists carefully uncover the bones and objects left behind by our ancestors. Studying these things helps us to understand how humans used to live.

PREHISTORIC ANIMALS

 The woolly mammoth was a large elephant-like mammal that lived about 350,000 years ago, during the last Ice Age. It had huge, curved tusks and a shaggy, two-layered coat to keep out the cold.

Sabre-toothed cats were muscular, with long, sharp canine teeth that they used for hunting. They became extinct about 12,500 years ago.

Mammoth

THROUGH THE AGES

 The points at which humans discovered new ways of making tools and weapons are divided into the following ages. Some civilizations made these important leaps earlier than others.

Stone Age

Early humans used stone to make tools and weapons.

The Stone Age is divided into three periods:

✦ Palaeolithic – the first stone tools were used. People lived in small groups, ate plants and hunted wild animals. Early works of art and religious rituals were created.

✦ Mesolithic – people lived in small groups, hunting and gathering food.

✦ Neolithic – people lived in bigger settlements. Farming and pottery were developed along with polished stone tools. The wheel was invented.

Bronze Age

Bronze, a mixture of copper and tin, was used to make weapons, tools and cooking utensils.

Iron Age

Iron began to replace bronze. Stronger tools helped farming to develop rapidly.

Evolution of humankind and animals

Until Victorian times, scientists believed species stayed the same. Charles Darwin showed that humans, animals and plants do change, due to what he called 'natural selection'. Plants and animals that have features best-suited to their environment are more likely to thrive and breed, passing these features on to their offspring. Over time, these features become more common in the species. This is called 'evolution'. Many Victorians were shocked by this idea and especially his daring suggestion that humans were animals and that we had evolved from apes!

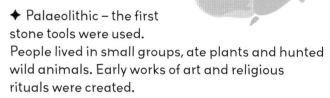

Around the world

There are 7 billion people and almost 200 countries in the world. Each country has its own languages, religions, cultures and races. Each also has its own jobs, food, education and laws.

THE CONTINENTS

A continent is a large, continuous mass of land consisting of a group of countries. There are seven continents:

1. Asia    **2.** Africa

3. North America   **4.** Europe

5. South America   **6.** Oceania

7. Antarctica

NORTH AMERICA

The first people to live in North America were the First Nations and the Inuit. North America includes the United States, Canada, the Arctic Circle and tiny Caribbean islands. Languages spoken include English, French, Spanish and Dutch. Coal mining and oil drilling are important industries here.

A fisherman in Canada, North America

I mine for coal in southern Africa.

SOUTH AMERICA

South America has the world's largest rainforest, the Amazon, and the second longest river, also called the Amazon. The world's longest mountain range, the Andes, runs for 8,900 km (5,500 miles) down the west coast. Most South Americans live in cities. The main languages are Spanish and Portuguese.

Brazil is the world's largest supplier of coffee.

ANTARCTICA

There isn't a permanent population on this freezing continent, because the icy conditions and harsh winds mean temperatures can drop as low as -80 °C! Most of the land is covered in ice. In mid-winter, the sun doesn't rise at all and in mid-summer it doesn't get dark. The only people to be found here are scientists who live in special research stations.

EUROPE

Europe is a rich continent with a high population. Goods produced here include crops and hi-tech services. Languages include English, French, German, Spanish and Italian. A total of 27 countries belong to the European Union (EU), making trade easier. Some of them share the same currency – the euro.

Grape-picking in France, Europe

I sell fruit and vegetables at a floating market in Bangkok.

ASIA

Asia is the world's biggest continent and has the most people. Some parts of Asia are very hot, such as India, and some are very cold, such as Siberia. Religions across Asia include Islam, Hinduism and Buddhism. China is one of the largest countries and its population is very large. Asia's biggest industries are manufacturing and oil production.

OCEANIA

This continent includes Australia, New Zealand and some small island countries. Australia has one of the lowest population densities in the world. Its centre is mainly desert, so most Australians live along the coast. The first people to live in Australia were called Aborigines and the first people to live in New Zealand were called Maoris. The countries make money by farming, mining gold, silver and diamonds and through tourism.

AFRICA

Africa has more than 50 countries and hundreds of different tribes. It has the longest river in the world, the Nile, and the largest desert, the Sahara. There are huge areas of forest and grasslands. Almost 2,000 different languages are spoken. Most people live around the Nile or on the coast, where the land is more fertile. Africa produces many foods such as fruit, as well as wine, minerals, and crops such as corn and wheat.

This is the world-famous Opera House in Sydney Harbour, Australia.

The history makers

History means all the events that have happened in the past. We find out about it through looking at things our ancestors left behind, such as books and the remains of buildings and objects.

ANCIENT AND MODERN

Ancient history includes things that happened up until AD476. Ancient history includes the ancient Egyptians, Vikings and Romans. From the 1500s onwards, it is called modern history. Modern history includes the World Wars, Victorian times and the Industrial Revolution. The Middle Ages is the time between these two periods. The key periods are shown in the timeline at the bottom of this page.

The pyramids at Giza, Egypt

The Parthenon, Athens

THE ANCIENT WORLD

Ancient Egypt

About 5,000 years ago, Ancient Egypt became a powerful kingdom. It was ruled by pharaohs. One of the best known is Tutankhamun, who became ruler as a boy. The statues and pyramids of Ancient Egypt were built as tombs for the pharaohs. The Great Pyramid, at Giza, took 20 years to build.

Ancient Greece

The ancient Greek civilization began about 4,000 years ago. Many important ideas about government, art and theatre came from the ancient Greeks. The Greeks built temples such as the Parthenon in Athens. They held the first Olympic Games and their mathematicians and scientists made great discoveries.

The Roman Empire

About 2,000 years ago, the Roman Empire ruled much of Europe and North Africa. Julius Caesar ruled Rome until he was murdered by his rivals. His adopted son, Octavian, then came to power as the first emperor, Augustus. The Romans built straight roads between cities, aqueducts, to carry water, and public baths. Some still exist today.

| Ancient Egypt c. 3000 BC | Ancient Greece c. 2000 BC | The Roman Empire c. 27 BC–AD 476 | The Middle Ages AD 476–1400s |

THE MIDDLE AGES

The Middle Ages began after the fall of the Roman Empire in AD 476. It was a time of great change in Europe. People were divided into groups, depending on their wealth and position in society. At the top were kings and queens, followed by nobles and lords, then knights who protected the land. At the bottom were peasants or 'serfs' who worked for lords in return for food and shelter.

Hello, I am a peasant and I work for my master in exchange for lodgings and food.

The Colosseum in Rome staged great gladiator battles and chariot races.

A Roman charioteer

THE MODERN WORLD

The Renaissance

From 1350 to 1600, Europe saw many discoveries in science, technology, art, music and the invention of the printing press. Great artists included Michelangelo, who painted the ceiling of the Sistine Chapel in Rome, and Leonardo da Vinci.

The Industrial Revolution

In the 1800s, major changes in agriculture and manufacturing spread across Europe, with advances in steam power, machine tools, transport, farming, mining and iron founding.

The World Wars

In the 20th century there were two world wars.
World War I – the Central Powers of Germany, Austria and Turkey fought against the Allies; the British Empire, France, Russia, Italy, Japan and the USA.
World War II – the Allies; the British Empire, the Soviet Union and USA, fought the Axis powers of Germany, Italy and Japan.
The Allies won both conflicts. Many weapons were used in these wars including tanks, bombs, fighter planes and poisonous gases. World War II was devastating and more than 50 million people were killed.

| The Renaissance 1350-1600 | The Industrial Revolution 1800s | World War I 1914-1918 | World War II 1939-1945 |

The human body

The human body is amazing! It can breathe, move, think and digest food and drink – all at the same time. We can keep our bodies healthy with a good diet and exercise.

THE SKELETON

The human skeleton, shown to the right, is made up of 206 bones. The largest is the femur, or thigh bone and the smallest is the stirrup bone, in the ear, which is about 2.5 mm long.

MUSCLES

Muscles expand and contract to make us move. The more we use them, the bigger and stronger they get. Bodybuilders have to work very hard to get the big muscles they have. The strongest muscles, called quadriceps, are in the legs.

> Some muscles work without us having to think about it – like our heart beating.

HEALTH & NUTRITION

Nutrients – These provide energy to maintain our bodies. The main sources are carbohydrates, protein, fat, vitamins and minerals.

Healthy Diet – Fruit and vegetables contain lots of fibre, which is very important for digestion. The human body also needs water to help it to work properly.

Exercise – People who exercise regularly tend to live longer and have much healthier lives.

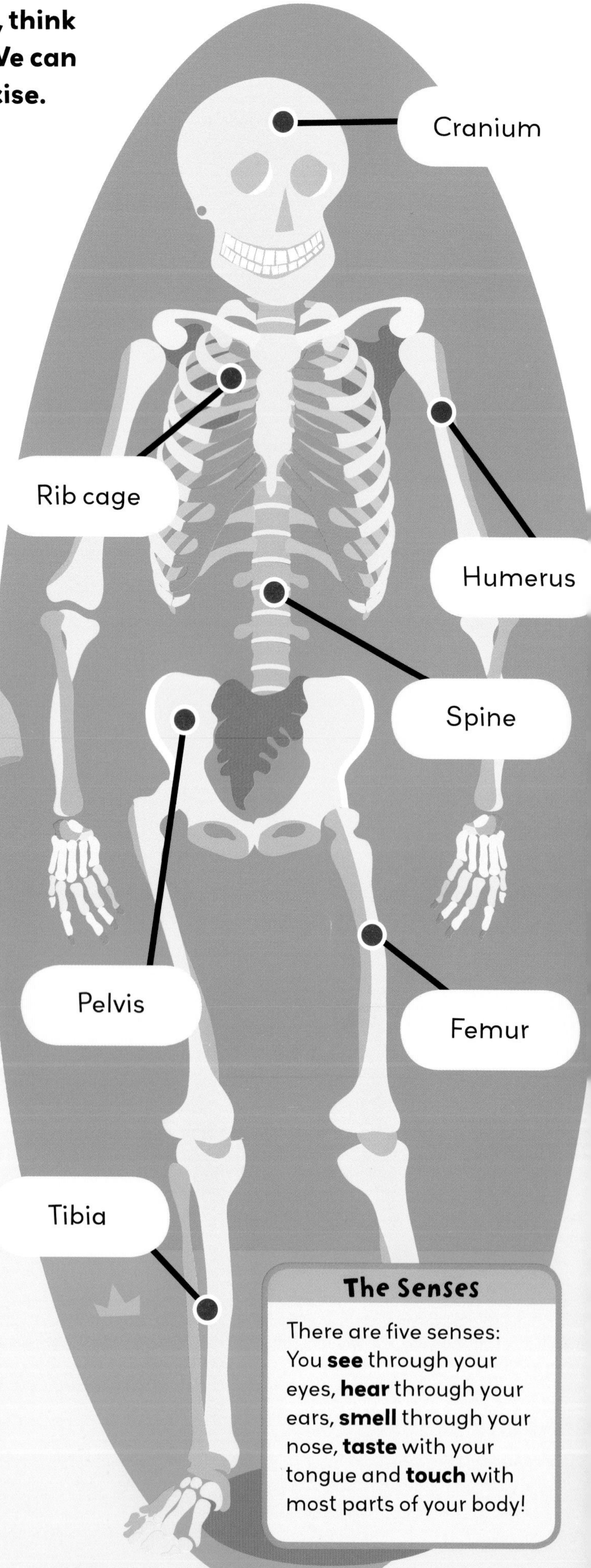

Cranium

Rib cage

Humerus

Spine

Pelvis

Femur

Tibia

The Senses

There are five senses: You **see** through your eyes, **hear** through your ears, **smell** through your nose, **taste** with your tongue and **touch** with most parts of your body!

Brain

SKIN

Your skin protects you, keeps you at the right temperature and gives you your sense of touch. There are three layers; the top layer makes new skin cells, to replace the ones that get rubbed off. The middle layer has nerve endings and tiny blood vessels. The bottom layer is made of fat and holds the skin to the muscles and bone underneath.

Heart

Lungs

Liver

Kidneys

ORGANS

Lungs – Contain 600 million tiny sacs called alveoli, which help oxygen to pass into your blood. They also get rid of carbon dioxide as you breathe out.

Heart – Made of muscle, pumping blood around the body, carrying oxygen and nutrients. It will beat almost 3 billion times in a lifetime and each day it pumps enough blood to fill a large paddling pool.

Brain – Contains a hundred billion nerve cells. It produces all your thoughts, movements, memories and emotions. Different parts specialise in different activities.

Kidneys – Process the blood to get rid of waste products and excess water. This flows to your bladder, which empties when you go to the loo.

Liver – Cleans the blood of toxins, and turns vitamins, sugar and fats into a form the body can use.

THE DIGESTIVE SYSTEM

After you chew your food and swallow, it travels down the gullet to the stomach, where it's churned with acid to turn it to mush. It goes through your intestines, which absorb the nutrients and water, and the leftover waste gets pushed out when you go to the loo. The whole system is up to 9 metres (30 feet) long and the process takes 1-3 days.

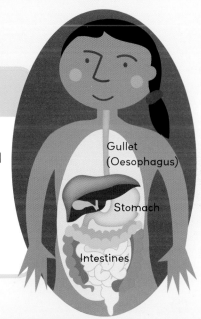

Gullet (Oesophagus)

Stomach

Intestines

Space and the Universe

Scientists believe that our universe began almost 14 billion years ago, with the 'big bang' – a huge explosion of energy and matter. The universe is still expanding today.

THE SOLAR SYSTEM

Our planet is one of nine that orbit the Sun, all in the same direction. The further planets are from the Sun, the slower they travel. They also have further to go to complete a whole cycle around the Sun.

So, Mercury orbits the Sun every three months but Neptune takes almost 165 years! Furthest from the Sun is Pluto, which was re-classified as a 'dwarf planet' in 2006. Other planets have moons, just like ours. In fact, Jupiter has 63 known moons!

This picture shows the order of the planets moving away from the Sun.

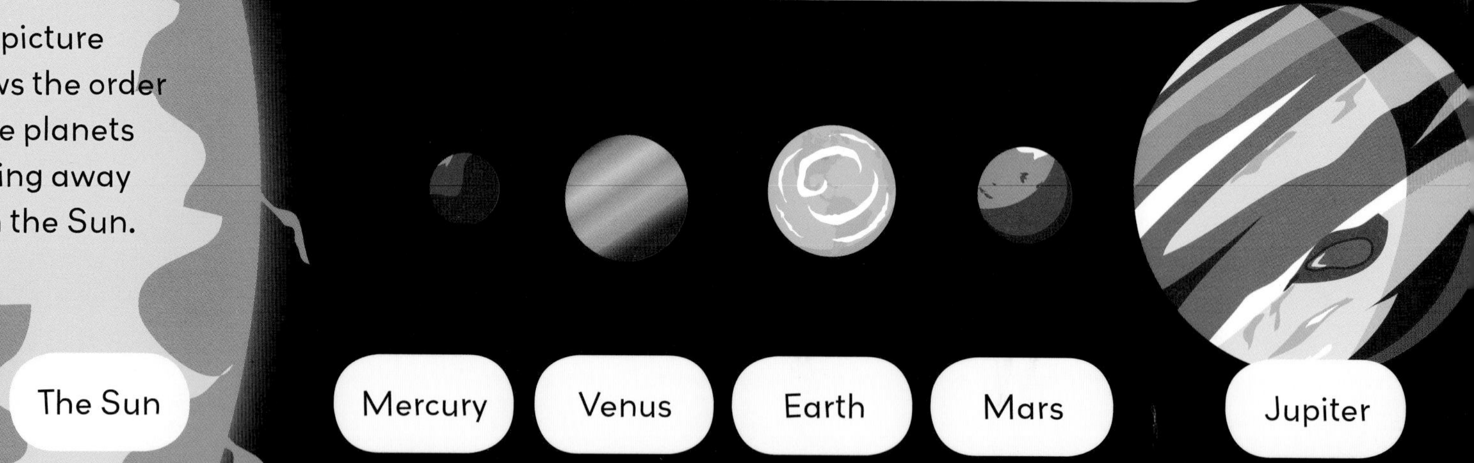

The Sun

Mercury

Venus

Earth

Mars

Jupiter

GALAXIES

The huge clusters of stars that fill the universe are known as galaxies. It is estimated that there are between 100 and 500 billion of them! Most are spiral or egg-shaped. Our own galaxy is a spiral galaxy called The Milky Way, with around 200–400 billion stars.

Gravity shaped gas and dust into vast clouds, which formed matter and, finally, stars.

FAMOUS ASTRONOMERS

Claudius Ptolemy (circa 100–170 AD) was the first astronomer to study the stars in a systematic way.

Nicholas Copernicus (1473–1543) discovered that the Earth revolves around the Sun.

Galileo Galilei (1564–1642) improved the telescope, saw craters on the Moon, moons around Jupiter and sunspots.

Johannes Kepler (1571–1630) discovered that all the planets revolve around the Sun.

Sir Isaac Newton (1643–1727) wrote his theory for the law of universal gravitation.

Edmund Halley (1656–1742) discovered that comets orbit the Sun. He predicted the return in 1758 of the comet named after him, Halley's Comet, which appears every 76 years.

Kepler

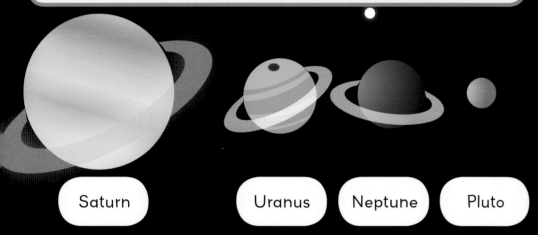

Saturn
Uranus
Neptune
Pluto

Moon Landing

In 1969, the American rocket Apollo 11 took the first humans to the Moon. Michael Collins piloted and Neil Armstrong and Edwin 'Buzz' Aldrin actually walked on the Moon's surface. Five more US missions successfully landed on the Moon, up until 1972. Some even included a kind of car, called a lunar rover.

Apollo 11

ROCKETS, SPACE STATIONS & SATELLITES

Rockets

The German V-2 was the first rocket to fly to the edge of space in 1942. In 1961, Russian spacecraft Vostok 1 was launched with the first human on board, cosmonaut Yuri Gagarin.

The first reusable spacecraft, the Space Shuttle, was launched by NASA, the American space agency, in 1982. It takes off attached to huge rockets, which drop off and later it glides back to earth.

Space Stations

In 1971, Salyut 1 became the first manned space station. The International Space Station (ISS) was completed in 2011. It is bigger than a full-sized soccer pitch. Astronauts from 14 countries have visited it.

Satellites

The first satellite to orbit Earth was the Russian Sputnik 1 in 1957. Satellites are used to help us to communicate and navigate. They monitor the weather and even spy on other countries!

All about weather

Weather is an endless cycle of events that includes wind, sunshine, rain and snow. It is the state of the air, or atmosphere, at any particular time or place.

Clouds

 Clouds are made up of tiny water droplets. They form when warm air rises, then cools, producing lots of water droplets, which create a cloud.

Rain

 Rain forms when water droplets in clouds stick together. When the droplets get really big and heavy, the cloud 'bursts' and it rains. There are lots of different types of rain, from light showers to torrential downpours.

Wind

 Wind is air moving from one place to another. The Sun warms the land. As air warms up, it rises and cold air moves in to take its place, causing wind.

Ice and Snow

 When water freezes, ice forms. It happens when its temperature drops below 0°C.

THE WATER CYCLE

The Earth has a certain amount of water that circulates on a journey up to the sky and back again. This constant movement of water is called 'the water cycle'.

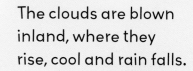

The clouds are blown inland, where they rise, cool and rain falls.

2

The water evaporates and rises into the air as water vapour, forming clouds.

1

Snow crystals form as water freezes in a cloud. As a crystal falls it hits others inside the cloud and becomes a snowflake.

Water in oceans, rivers and lakes is heated by the Sun.

EXTREME WEATHER

Extreme weather can have devastating effects – floods where there is too much water and droughts where there is not enough. Hurricanes and tornadoes can leave people starving, homeless or even dead.

3

As rain falls, it flows into rivers, then back into the sea.

4

WHAT IS CLIMATE?

Weather refers to the conditions we see over a fairly short period of time. 'Climate' is the pattern of weather conditions over a long period of time. Climates vary across the world. They depend upon distance from the Equator, position on a continent, how high the land is and how close it is to water.

Far away from the Equator, the climate is always cold.

Ocean currents carry warm water to cooler parts of the Earth.

WHAT IS GLOBAL WARMING?

Global warming is the rise in temperature of the Earth's atmosphere. The atmosphere is made up of layers of natural gases called 'greenhouse gases'.

Humans are increasing the warming of the Earth through pollution. Producing too much carbon dioxide by burning coal and oil, and destroying the forests that absorb carbon dioxide, is creating extra greenhouse gases. These extra gases hold in more heat, making the planet warmer.

Greenhouse gases trap heat, keeping the Earth warm

Some sunlight that hits the Earth is reflected

Atmosphere

Plants

There are millions of different types of plant in the world, and we use them for lots of things, including food, medicine and clothes. Plants are the key to life on Earth; without them we wouldn't exist.

HOW PLANTS GROW

Most flowering plants start as seeds, or bulbs in the ground. In the right conditions, a seed cracks open and a root grows down into the soil. This holds the plant in place and takes in nutrients and water. Next, a green shoot emerges from the soil and leaves grow. Then buds appear, which open as flowers.

Pollination

Plants reproduce in a process called pollination. Pollen from one plant is transferred to another, which fertilises the plant. Nearly all pollination is done by insects and bees. Pollen gets caught on the insect's body and rubs off on to other plants. The wind also transfers pollen.

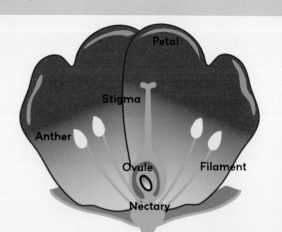

Petal
Stigma
Anther
Ovule
Filament
Nectary

WHAT PLANTS NEED

Plants take water and nutrients from the ground and turn these into food to help them to grow. They need plenty of sunlight and carbon dioxide, which they make into food in a process called photosynthesis. Most plants grow best in wet soil where there is lots of sunlight. Some, such as the cactus, grow in very hot, dry places. Others, like moss and lichen, grow on rocks or on other plants.

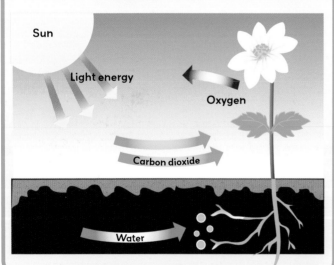

Sun
Light energy
Oxygen
Carbon dioxide
Water

Seed

Root

Many plants have flowers which grow from the stem. They often smell nice!

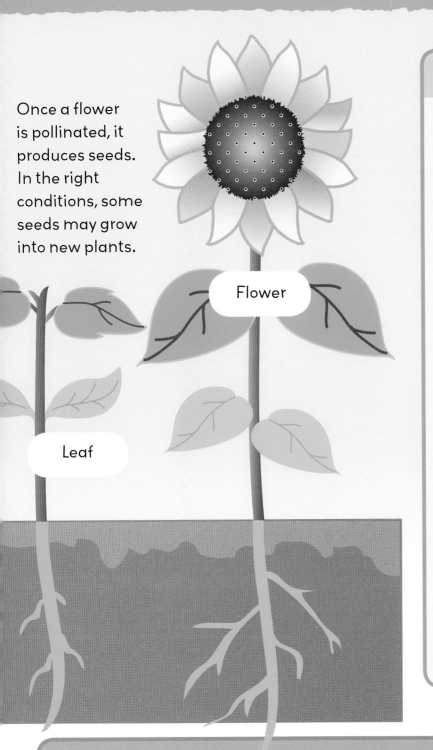

Once a flower is pollinated, it produces seeds. In the right conditions, some seeds may grow into new plants.

Flower

Leaf

TREES

Trees are very important to the environment. Some have leaves that go brown and fall off in the autumn. These are called 'deciduous' trees. 'Evergreen' trees have leaves that stay green all year round.

Trees produce oxygen and they also provide homes for many animals. We use trees for lots of things, from making paper to using wood to build furniture and homes.

Trees have a stem just like smaller plants do. The stem of a tree is called a trunk. A trunk has arms or branches, which grow leaves. Leaves come in many different shapes, sizes and colours. They can have rounded, soft edges, or be hard and prickly. Some are long and thin, like a needle.

Pine needles and cone

Oak leaf

Holly leaf

SELF DEFENCE

Some plants have thorns and stings that help to protect them. The thorns on the stem of a rose and the stings on a stinging nettle can help to protect the delicate plant from animals that might damage or eat it.

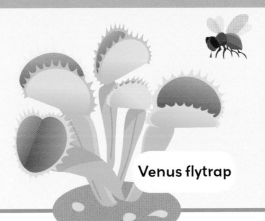

Venus flytrap

Carnivorous plants

Some plants, such as the Venus flytrap, can catch insects. When an insect lands on the open leaves of the Venus flytrap, tiny hairs sense its movement and the trap snaps shut. Digestive juices break down the insect and the plant absorbs the nutrients.

Animals

Scientists divide animals into types, depending on how their bodies work. Some animals are wild, or untamed by humans, and others are domesticated, such as pets or farm animals.

MAMMALS

Mammals have a backbone and are warm-blooded. They have hair on their body and sweat glands. Females produce milk to feed their young. Most mammals give birth to their young, but some, such as the platypus, lay eggs instead.

BIRDS

Birds have a backbone and are warm-blooded. They have two legs and a pair of wings. Their bodies are covered in feathers and they lay eggs, instead of giving birth to their young. Most birds can fly but some, such as ostriches and penguins, have lost the ability to fly.

FISH

Fish are usually cold-blooded, with a backbone and fins, which they use to swim in water. They have scales and they breathe using gills. There are many species of fish and nearly all live in water, either in the sea or in ponds, lakes or rivers.

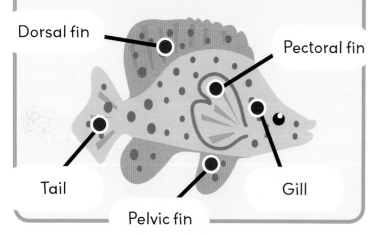

Dorsal fin

Pectoral fin

Tail

Gill

Pelvic fin

ENDANGERED

Some 'endangered' animals are threatened with extinction, meaning that they could die out completely. This may be due to hunting or loss of their natural habitat or food supply. Tigers, pandas, polar bears and gorillas are all endangered. There are many projects that aim to protect them from extinction.

INSECTS

Insects are invertebrates, meaning that they have no internal backbone. Instead, they have a hard outer skeleton called an 'exoskeleton'. They have six jointed legs and their bodies are divided into three parts; the head, thorax and abdomen. Insects belong to the group of invertebrates called arthropods. Many arthropods are mistakenly called insects. Spiders and scorpions are arachnids, meaning that they have eight legs and that their bodies are fused together in one part, instead of being broken up into sections like an insect's. They don't have wings or antennae.

REPTILES

Reptiles have a backbone and are cold-blooded. They have scaly skin and most lay eggs. Reptiles lay their eggs on land, unlike amphibians. They heat their bodies by spending time in the sun. Reptiles come in all shapes and sizes and there are four types:

◆ Snakes and lizards
◆ Crocodile family
◆ Tuatara (which look like lizards)
◆ Turtles and tortoises

It is believed that Tui Malila, a tortoise given to the Tongan royal family by Captain Cook in 1777, was the grand old age of 188 when she died in 1965.

People who study and observe animals are called zoologists.

AMPHIBIANS

Amphibians have a backbone and are cold-blooded. Many people confuse them with reptiles, but they are very different. Instead of scales they have smooth, wet skin, which they breathe through. They often live near water or damp places and they usually lay their eggs straight into water. Amphibians include frogs, toads, newts and salamanders.

World's resources

The world provides us with many different resources, some of which we need to live and to stay healthy, and others that make our lives more comfortable or more enjoyable.

This picture shows lots of different ways of generating energy; including solar, nuclear, wind, coal, tidal and hydro-electric power.

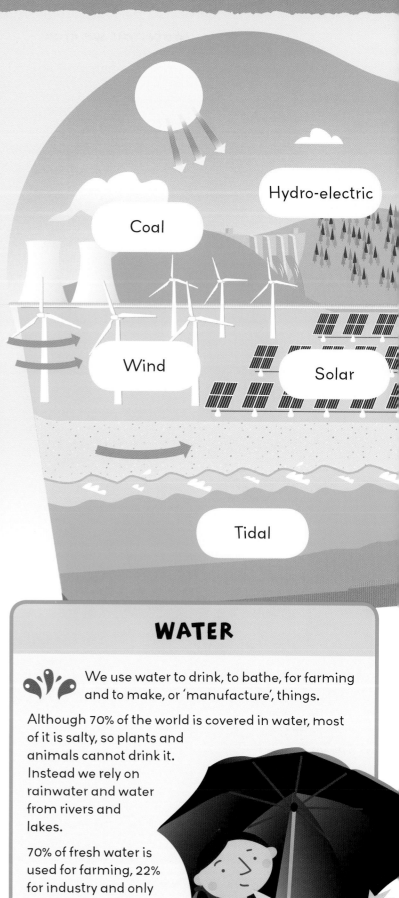

Hydro-electric

Coal

Wind

Solar

Tidal

ENERGY

We use energy for all these things:

✦ To keep us warm – fires and central heating; or to keep us cool – air conditioning

✦ To cook and refrigerate food

✦ To travel – cars, lorries, aeroplanes, trains, ships

✦ For lighting, in buildings and outside

✦ For making things we use every day, like TVs

We get energy from non-renewable sources which we use up and cannot replace, and also from renewable sources which we can replace, or which replace themselves.

Non-renewable Sources

These include oil, coal and gas. We use oil to make fuel for transport, and we use coal and gas to keep us warm. All of them are used to make the electricity that powers many of the things we use every day. The problems are that these resources are running out and the fumes they give off damage the environment and increase global warming.

Renewable Sources

Turbines harness wind energy and solar panels capture energy from the Sun. We can also use tidal power and river, or hydro-electric, power. Plants can be used to make biofuels for cars. Wood is a renewable form of fuel, but it takes years to grow and burning it increases global warming. Nuclear power is cleaner. It is used to generate electricity, but it costs a lot to set up and many people worry about the risk of leaks.

WATER

We use water to drink, to bathe, for farming and to make, or 'manufacture', things.

Although 70% of the world is covered in water, most of it is salty, so plants and animals cannot drink it. Instead we rely on rainwater and water from rivers and lakes.

70% of fresh water is used for farming, 22% for industry and only 8% for home use. In hot, dry countries, they use almost all their water to grow food.

Some countries have lots of rain and some get very little.

MATERIALS

Materials we grow

✦ Cotton, wool and linen, for clothing

✦ Wood, for buildings, furniture and paper

✦ Hemp, for cloth and rope

✦ Rubber, for tyres, hoses and footwear

Materials we get from the ground

✦ Rocks, such as stone and slate, for floors and roofs

✦ Clay, for bricks

✦ Metals, especially iron

✦ Sand, for making glass

✦ Oil, for making plastic

> I drill for oil, which can be made into petrol for cars.

Nuclear

FOOD

 Every year, we produce four billion tonnes of food:

✦ Fruit and vegetables – 1.4 billion

✦ Meat and dairy products, such as milk and cheese – 0.7 billion

✦ Seafood, mainly fish – 0.1 billion

✦ Staples; bread, rice, cereal, potatoes – 1.2 billion

✦ Sugar – 0.2 billion

✦ Other foods, such as tea, coffee, spices – 0.3 billion

Sharing the Food

While many countries in the world have plenty of food, millions of people in poorer countries do not have enough. In developed countries, food production is industrialised and uses expensive machinery and large tracts of land. In poorer countries, much of the farming is still carried out on small family plots, without the use of machinery.

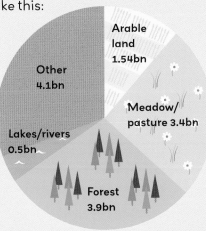

In some developing countries, often with very hot, dry climates, it is difficult to grow enough food. Sometimes, if there is not enough rainfall, the crops do not grow and many people do not have any food. This leads to a famine.

LAND

 There are 13.5 billion hectares of land in the world, which is just under two hectares per person. That's equivalent to nine American football pitches for a family of four people! The land gets used like this:

Some countries are more crowded than others – you could fit Japan into Australia 21 times, but it has six times as many people! Some countries have land that it is easier to grow food on.

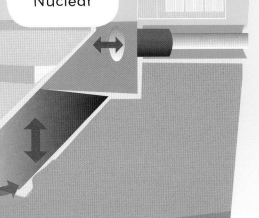

Arable land 1.54bn

Other 4.1bn

Meadow/pasture 3.4bn

Lakes/rivers 0.5bn

Forest 3.9bn

Science and technology

The aim of science is to discover things about the world and how it works. Scientific knowledge constantly changes. Scientists hope this helps us to improve our understanding of how things work.

WHAT DO SCIENTISTS DO?

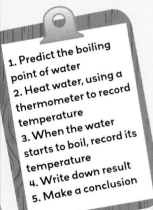

Scientists have lots of ways of finding out about things.

Experiments – step-by-step processes that scientists set up to test their ideas. They start with a prediction, or 'hypothesis' of what might happen, then they conduct research to give them information. So, if a scientist wanted to know the boiling point of water, she might conduct this experiment:

1. Predict the boiling point of water
2. Heat water, using a thermometer to record temperature
3. When the water starts to boil, record its temperature
4. Write down result
5. Make a conclusion

Scientists use evidence from experiments to prove their hypotheses.

Atoms

All things are made up of tiny particles called atoms – the building blocks for everything in the universe.

SOLIDS, LIQUIDS AND GASES

Materials are divided into states depending on what form they take.

Solids – made up of parts that are joined together and have a fixed shape. A rock is a solid.

Liquids – made of parts that are joined together but can move around so they flow and have no fixed shape. Water is a liquid.

Gases – made of parts that can float freely in air. Oxygen is a gas.

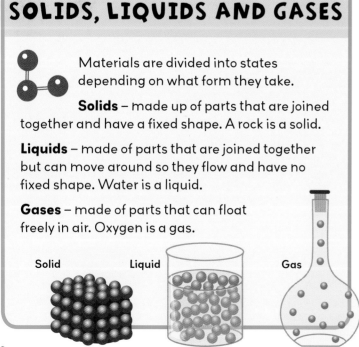

Solid   Liquid   Gas

CHEMICAL, PHYSICAL AND BIOLOGICAL

Science is split into three main areas:

Chemistry studies the elements that form all of the world's substances. It looks at the structure of substances and how they combine together to make other substances.

Physics studies the properties and nature of material. It looks at energy – heat, light, sound – and the ways materials and energy interact. It also studies electricity, magnets and radioactive things.

Biology studies living things and how they work. It looks at the human body, animals and plants.

Electricity

Electricity is made up of tiny parts of atoms called electrons that are positive or negative. When they move they create electricity.

ENERGY

Sound, light and heat are all forms of energy. Energy is the ability to do work. Energy is stored in fuels, as chemicals in food and in batteries. When certain chemical reactions occur, energy is released and this makes things happen. For example, when petrol in a car engine is heated it starts to burn and releases energy to power the pistons that make the car move.

MAGNETS

Magnets have two poles – a north pole at one end and a south pole at the other. Opposite poles create a force that pulls them together. This means that they **attract** each other. Two poles that are the same – two north poles or two south poles – create a force that pushes them apart. This means they **repel** each other.

Iron is a magnetic metal, but copper and gold are not.

FORCES

Forces are pushes and pulls in a certain direction. They determine the shape and movement of an object. If the forces on each side of an object are equal, the object will stay still or if it is already moving it will carry on the same as before.

Unbalanced forces (where one force is stronger than the other), change the way something is moving. If there is an unbalanced force, an object will either start to move, speed up, slow down or change direction.

Force is measured in units called newtons (N).

Gravity is the force that makes things fall to the ground and keeps them on Earth.

Communication

Communication can be divided into two types: communication that uses sound, such as speech or music, and communication that does not use sound, such as pictures, body or sign language.

Television

Post

Telephone

TYPES OF COMMUNICATION

Language is one of the main ways people communicate. It can be both spoken and written and each language has its own system of signs and symbols. There are many languages spoken in the world.

Sign language and Braille are used by people who are deaf or blind. Sign language uses hand movements and facial expressions to mean different things. The Braille alphabet is made up of different shapes of raised dots, which people feel with their fingers to read.

Ancient languages such as Hebrew, Greek and Latin are the basis for many languages used today, and have influenced many words that we use.

Early Communication

Before computers, the Internet and mobile phones were around, people had to rely on more simple methods of communication. Early man started to create art, such as cave drawings, to describe events and objects around them. Before written language was widespread, people would tell stories aloud to pass knowledge down the generations.

Animal Language

Animals use simple sounds and actions to communicate with each other.

BODY LANGUAGE

Our bodies are communicating with other people all the time without us even realising it. Facial expressions, the way we are sitting, our tone of voice and our hand movements all show our feelings to other people.

Computer

Radio

TELEPHONE

Telephones were invented in the 1870s, to help people communicate. Landline telephones use a wire to connect the phone to a telephone network. Mobile phones convert sound waves from the caller's voice into electrical signals. These are transmitted as radio waves and sent by aerial or satellite to the person being called.

Mobile phones have transformed people's lives – almost five billion people use them worldwide.

Newspaper

MEDIA

TV, radio and newspapers allow news to be shared quickly and easily. In many parts of the world, there is 24-hour coverage, so people can follow important things, such as politics and sporting events, as they are happening.

In the past, news would be read out by a town crier in every town square. Most people would not be able to hear what they said and news would take a long time to travel around a country.

It is now possible to make a phone call from almost anywhere in the world.

COMPUTERS & THE INTERNET

The invention of computers and the Internet changed the world. In 1991, the World Wide Web was introduced to the public and the Internet as we know it was born.

Around a quarter of the world's population now uses the Internet for communicating with each other, learning, shopping, banking, playing games and much more. The Internet makes it easy for people to share knowledge and to communicate with other people anywhere in the world.

Getting around

We use transport to take people and goods from one place to another. Many people use land transport such as a car or motorbike every day. There are also ways of travelling in the air, on water and by rail.

ON THE TRACKS

A train is a group of linked carriages that are pulled along a metal track by an engine. Trains carry passengers and heavy loads. The TGV is an electric train in France. It travels at a speed of about 320 km (200 miles) an hour. The fastest train in the world is the Maglev. The train floats above a special magnetic track and its record speed is 581 km (361 miles) an hour.

Lots of cities have underground rail systems.

ON THE ROAD

There are more than 500 million cars on the road, of all different shapes and sizes, from tiny hatchback cars to huge four-wheel drives. Many people use a car every day to travel to work. Cars have an engine, body and four wheels. Most cars are powered by petrol or diesel. The engine burns the fuel to make the car move, creating fumes which pollute the environment. Nowadays, people can buy electric cars or hybrids, which are powered by fuel and electricity. These cars are better for the environment.

Other vehicles on the road include motorbikes and bicycles. Lorries, trucks and vans are large vehicles used by industry to transport goods.

Special cars are built to race against each other. They have a streamlined design to make them go fast. Racing cars, such as Formula One cars, can travel at speeds of nearly 400 km (248 miles) an hour – that's more than 100 metres in only a second!

Hi, I'm a courier. I drive a van and I deliver parcels to homes and businesses.

IN THE AIR

An aeroplane is a vehicle that carries people from one place to another in the air. It has two wings and usually two or four engines. The plane is flown by a pilot who sits at the front, in the cockpit.

Jumbo jets are passenger planes that can carry up to 600 people. Other types of air transport include helicopters, gliders and supersonic jets. Helicopters can get to places that other vehicles cannot reach, so are often used in emergencies. Supersonic jets fly very fast and they are often used in air battles. In the future, even faster jets could be used to transport people.

How a jet engine works

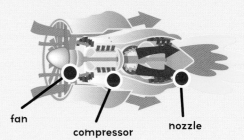

fan compressor nozzle

The engine sucks air in through a fan at the front. Blades compress the air, then it's sprayed with fuel and ignited by an electric spark. The burning gases expand and blast out through the nozzle, pushing the aircraft forward.

ON THE WATER

Boats and ships have been used to transport goods for thousands of years. They once used sails and wind power to move. Nowadays, large boats and ships are powered by an engine that burns fuel.

There are many different kinds of water transport, from small speedboats and yachts to ferry boats and large cruise ships that carry thousands of people. Some ships also carry goods from one country to another. They are called cargo ships. A hovercraft is a speedy boat that sits on a cushion of air. It can travel on land and on water.

Some people try to break world speed records in boats. Some boats go faster than Formula One racing cars. They have jet engines and reach speeds of more than 500 km (310 miles) an hour. Other people have sailed around the world in a boat – the world record time for this is only 71 days, which is very fast!

Sport and games

There are hundreds of types of sport, played by individuals and teams. There are games with balls, racing competitions with cars, bikes and horses, and sports that test strength, agility and balance.

BALL GAMES

Basketball, baseball, rugby, cricket, American football, netball and football are all team ball games. In football, there are usually two teams of 11 players. Every four years, 32 teams from countries around the world compete against each other in the football World Cup.

Some sports are played with much smaller balls, such as snooker, tennis or golf. Golf is played with a small ball and a long stick called a club. Players take turns to hit the ball into a hole on a course of nine or 18 holes. Whoever takes the fewest shots wins.

Hi, I play football, which is the world's most popular sport.

OLYMPIC GAMES

The Olympic Games began in ancient Greece in 776 BC. The Summer Olympics are now held every four years, in a different country each time, with top athletes from all around the world taking part.

In the Summer Olympics there are 26 sports, with over 300 events, including swimming and diving, athletics, basketball, canoeing, cycling, boxing, show jumping, gymnastics, judo, volleyball and weightlifting. There are also paralympic sports, which are played by people with disabilities.

The Winter Olympics are also held every four years. Sports include skiing, curling, the bobsleigh, ice hockey and snowboarding.

JUICE!

TOUGH STUFF

In some sports, people take turns to get the best score and then the scores are compared against each other.

In weightlifting, the competitors lift as much weight as they can. Darts players take it in turns to throw darts at a scoreboard. Divers dive into the pool and are scored by judges. Ice skaters and gymnasts also perform in front of judges where they must put on a special show, with spectacular twists, jumps and turns.

Some sports focus on endurance, meaning that they test strength and stamina over a long period of time. Long-distance running, rowing, cross-country skiing and triathlon are all endurance sports. Triathlon has three parts: swimming, cycling and running, all completed one after the other in a single day!

Hi, I am a figure skater. I perform my routines for the judges and hope that they will award me top marks!

THE RACE IS ON

Some sports take place at a track, or circuit, using racing cars, motorbikes, bicycles or horses. Formula One uses racing cars, which zoom around a track. Nascar is a popular motorsport in the United States. It uses specially-built cars, which have reached speeds of 341 km (212 miles) an hour.

Other racing sports take place on a different type of circuit. Cycling races often use ordinary roads or paths. The famous Tour de France lasts for three weeks and covers around 3,600 km (2,200 miles) of different terrains, from flat to hilly and even mountainous.

Art

Art is one of the ways people can express their feelings and thoughts. There are many forms of art, including painting, sculpture, music, literature and film.

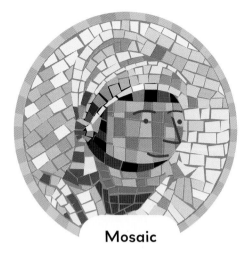

Mosaic

French Impressionism

EARLY ART

The oldest pieces of art were scratched out of stone, bone and shells over 70,000 years ago. Some cave paintings date back more than 30,000 years.

The ancient Egyptians used painting in their religious ceremonies. Sometimes they carved pictures into rock and they also made fine pottery and jewellery. Later the ancient Greeks and Romans used more realistic art – many of their statues, carvings, mosaics and pottery still exist.

THE RENAISSANCE

The 'Renaissance' period, which started in the 1400s in Italy, was a golden age as art became more realistic.

Two famous artists of this time were Michelangelo and Leonardo da Vinci. During the Renaissance, the development of printing allowed books to be produced more easily. Pictures in books were made using woodcuts – images carved into wood, like a potato stamp. The artist Albrecht Durer produced some of the finest woodcuts of this time.

Michelangelo

In the Middle Ages, art was usually found in churches, in stained glass and in books.

ART MEDIA

Before the Renaissance, most painting was done by mixing a coloured powder, called a **pigment**, with water, to make a paste. For smaller pictures, egg was mixed with the pigment, instead of water, to make **tempera**. **Oil painting** was developed in Holland around 1420. It was more colourful and easier to use than tempera. Venice had a lot of sail-canvas, so oil painting on canvas became popular there. Canvas is still widely used today. **Watercolour** painting became popular around 1800, particularly amongst amateur painters. In the 1950s, much brighter **acrylic** paints were developed. Other types of drawing, using **pencil**, **crayon**, or **pen and ink**, are used for detailed effects.

Wall painting

Renaissance art

Post-impressionism

Abstract art

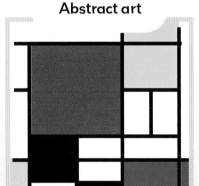

Mosaics use lots of small pieces of glass or pottery to make a picture.

MODERN & CONTEMPORARY

Modern art is said to have started around 1860, with the French **Impressionists**, who concentrated on the effects of light and colour. Famous Impressionists included Monet, Renoir, Degas, Cezanne and Manet. Other artists – the '**Post-impressionists**' – produced pictures that were even less realistic, but more colourful and intense, such as Vincent van Gogh, Gauguin and Seurat.

From the 1890s, **Art Nouveau** developed, applying natural, flowing shapes to art and architecture. The Paris Metro entrances still display their original art nouveau designs.

Cezanne

In the new century, the **Fauvists**, such as Matisse, used a lot of colour.

The **Expressionists**, who emerged in Germany around 1910, sought to convey emotion above all else. **Cubism** also became popular, where all sides of an object are shown, as in Picasso's work. By the 1920s, the **Surrealists**, including Magritte and Dalí, painted art to confuse and surprise the viewer. **Abstract** artists, such as Jackson Pollock and Mondrian, concentrated on patterns and colours.

Art after World War II is generally referred to as **Contemporary art**. It includes a wide range of artists all trying to do very different things.

Pop Art uses modern everyday objects to comment on modern life. Andy Warhol and David Hockney are famous for their pop art. Some abstract artists developed a style called **minimalism**, in which a picture would have very little in it. The artists believed 'less is more'.

Sculpture is three-dimensional artwork made using materials such as stone, clay, metal, wood or glass. Rodin's The Thinker, right, is a very famous sculpture. There are copies on show in museums all around the world.

Index

This book was conceived and created by iSeek Ltd, RH17 5PA www.iseekcreative.com